HUMAN BODY FACT FRENZY!

.... by Cari Meister ....

CAPSTONE PRESS
a capstone imprint

Published by Capstone Press, an imprint of Capstone
1710 Roe Crest Drive, North Mankato, Minnesota 56003
capstonepub.com

Human Body Fact Frenzy! was originally published as *Wacky Facts About the Human Body*, copyright 2016 by Capstone Press.

Copyright © 2026 by Capstone. All rights reserved. No part of this publication may be reproduced in whole or in part, or stored in a retrieval system, or transmitted in any form or by any means, electronic, mechanical, photocopying, recording, or otherwise, without written permission of the publisher.

Library of Congress Cataloging-in-Publication Data is available
on the Library of Congress website.
ISBN: 9798875233760 (hardcover)
ISBN: 9798875233715 (paperback)
ISBN: 9798875233722 (ebook PDF)

Summary: Readers will love this collection of human body facts featuring browsable text and unexpected photos!

Editorial Credits
Editor: Alison Deering; Designers: Jaime Willems and Tracy Davies; Media Researcher: Svetlana Zhurkin; Production Specialist: Whitney Schaefer

Image Credits
CDC: James Gathany, 31; Getty Images: 3bugsmom, 4 (middle), Ben Gingell, 4 (right), 32, eugenesergeev, 34, Image Source, 60, Imgorthand, 42, Ljupco, 1 (bottom), 52, NinaMalyna, 35 (bottom), Roxana Wegner, 6, ruizluquepaz, 24, Science Photo Library/Sciepro, 21, SeventyFour, 12, yumiyum, 17, Zinkevych, 25; Shutterstock: Agnieszka Karpinska (human organs), 3 and throughout, Alena Ivochkina, 4 (left), AlexandrBognat, 20 (top), Alioui Ma, 44, Altrendo Images, 62, Ana Krasavina (arrows and lines), 8 and throughout, Anatoliy Karlyuk, 27, Andrii Oleksiienko, 9, antoniodiaz, 8, Ao win, cover (nose), Athiyada's, 35, AYO Production, 59, bescec, 16 (top), 20 (bottom), bestv, 11, Boris Riaposov, 61, Carlos Caetano, 45 (front), Cast Of Thousands, 33 (bottom), 46 (middle), Cat Simpson, 22, Chiari VFX, 36 (front), Chris Curtis, 5 (middle), CkyBe (speech bubbles), cover and throughout, Creative Travel Projects, 26, crystal light, 18, daniyalpro, 1 (top), 7 (middle), Elena Pimukova (rays), 6 and throughout, Explode, 14, Flashon Studio, 51 (middle), Fotoluminate LLC, 23, Gajus, 39, gn8 (rays and lines), cover and throughout, Ground Picture, 5 (top and bottom), 10 (bottom), Guppic the duck, cover (crown, glasses), IdeaGeneration (brain), cover, back cover, Jacek Chabraszewski, 29 (top), Kateryna Kon, 48, Kaynur.ry, 41, KhalilahOne, 33 (top), Kjpargeter, 15, Konstantin Labunskiy, 40, Magic mine, 38, MattL_Images, 19, Maya Kruchankova, 50, metamorworks, 57 (boy), Mikhail Dudarev, 13, My Stockers, cover (lungs, heart), Net Vector (slime), 36, 45, New Africa, 29 (bottom), Olkita, 30 (top), ONYXprj, 46 (top), Pixel-Shot, 10 (middle), Pressmaster, 54 (top), Prostock-studio, cover (hands), 37, 54 (bottom), 63, 64, Puwadol Jaturawutthichai, 53, Roman Samborskyi, 43, 56, Rommel Canlas, 55, Sinhyu Photographer, 16 (lung tissue), smx12, 16 (magnifying glass), sruilk, 28, Suan Taang, 47, Team Pre-Light, 58, Top Vector Studio (background icons), cover, back cover, v_kulieva (gradient background), back cover and throughout, Valdis Skudre, 51 (top), W.Y. Sunshine, 49

Any additional websites and resources referenced in this book are not maintained, authorized, or sponsored by Capstone. All product and company names are trademarks™ or registered® trademarks of their respective holders.

Printed and bound in the USA. PO 6307

Table of Contents

A Head-to-Toe Collection of Body Facts **4**

Awesome Organs **6**

In Your Face **22**

Sweat, Gas, Mucus, and More **36**

Stretch, Stand, Move **50**

A HEAD-TO-TOE COLLECTION OF BODY FACTS

You pump up your bike tires when they are low. You fill a car up with gas to make it go. You plug in your phone to charge it. But what do you do to take care of your body? Your bones are stronger than concrete and your body contains more than 60,000 miles (96,561 kilometers) of blood vessels, so it's time to learn and appreciate what your body does for you.

AWESOME ORGANS

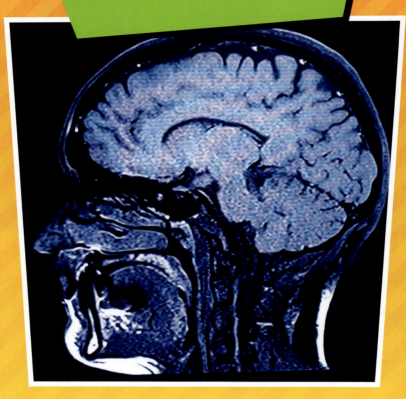

Your brain has about 100 billion neurons in it.

About 80 percent of your brain is water.

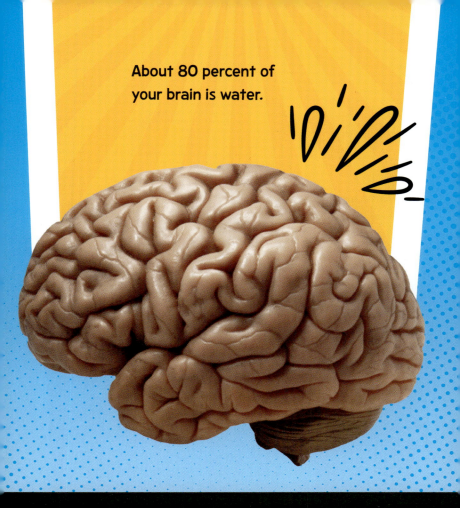

Your brain has more fat on it than any other organ.

Skin is your body's largest organ.

The average person sheds about 44 pounds (20 kilograms) of skin in a lifetime.

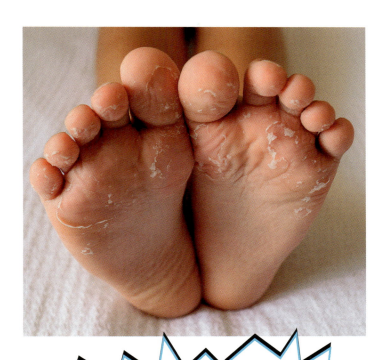

WOW!

THE TOP LAYER OF YOUR SKIN IS DEAD CELLS.

Your kidneys look like giant kidney beans.

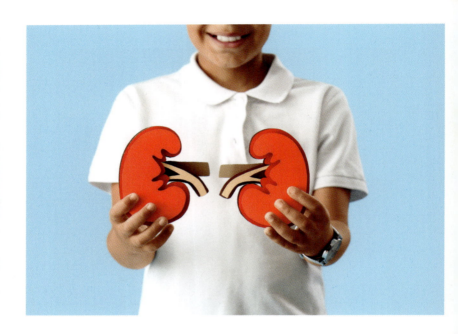

They're about 4 inches (10 centimeters) long, or about the length of your hand.

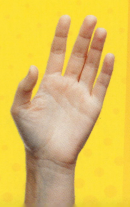

Kidneys filter about 50 gallons (189 liters) of blood per day.

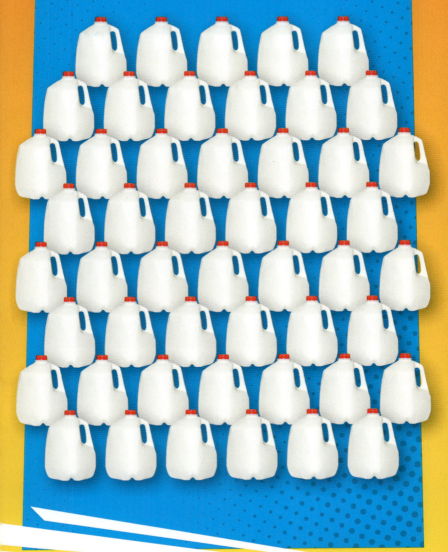

The heart beats about 100,000 times a day.

An average human heart will beat about 2.5 billion times in a lifetime.

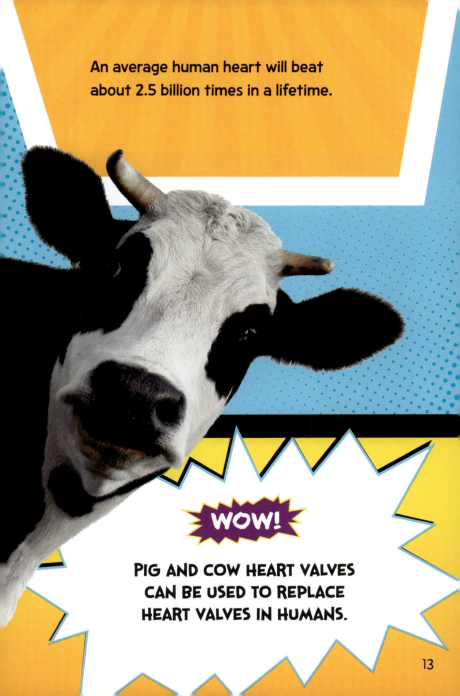

WOW!

PIG AND COW HEART VALVES CAN BE USED TO REPLACE HEART VALVES IN HUMANS.

A heart can beat outside a body for a short time.

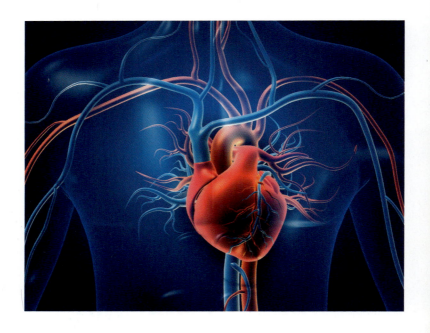

A heart pumps about 1.5 million barrels of blood during a lifetime.

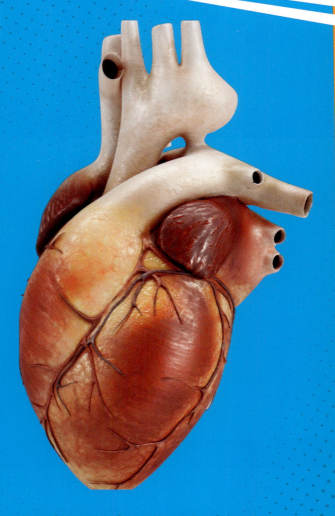

Your heart isn't really red. It's a red-brown color with patches of yellow fat.

Lungs are spongy. They are the only organs that can float on water.

The left lung is smaller
than the right lung.

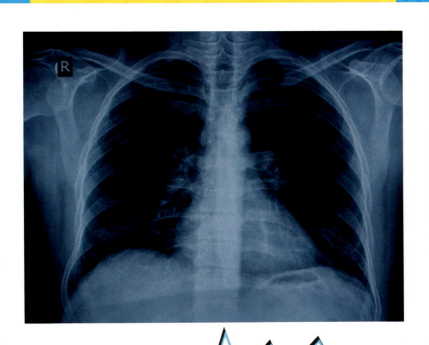

YOU CAN LIVE WITH ONE LUNG.

Your liver is shaped like a football with a flat top.

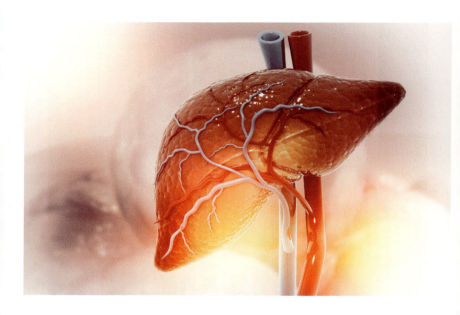

At 3.5 pounds (1.6 kg), the liver wins the title for the heaviest internal organ.

The liver does about 500 different jobs, such as cleaning blood and storing energy.

A pancreas is shaped like a skinny sock.

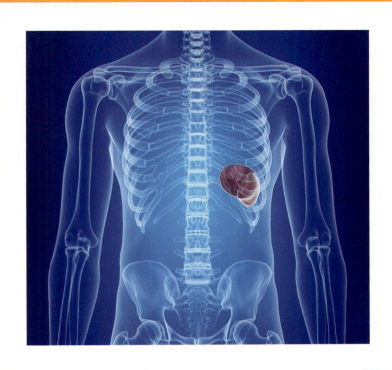

Your spleen is soft, purple, and about the size of your fist.

You can live without your spleen.

IN YOUR FACE

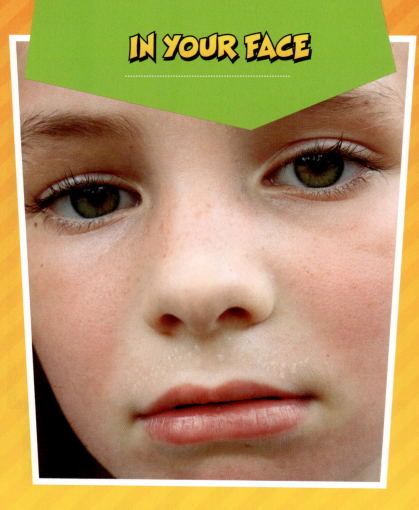

Lips do not have sweat glands, so they do not sweat.

The blood underneath the skin makes lips look red.

Lips have more than 1 million nerve endings, so they are very sensitive.

Your lips get thinner as you get older.

Every tongue print is unique.

You have about 9,000 taste buds on your tongue.

Your tongue is one of the strongest muscles in your body.

Humans can see about 10 million different colors.

Some people can hear their eyeballs moving.

Exophthalmos is a condition in which a person's eyeballs bulge.

Some people are born without irises, or the colored part of the eye.

Some people have two rows of eyelashes.

Your eyes are made mostly of a jellylike goop.

You blink about 6,205,000 times in one year.

It is impossible to keep your eyes open when you sneeze.

A sneeze can travel up to 100 miles per hour (161 kilometers per hour).

The nose can detect about 1 trillion different smells.

Your ears and nose never stop growing.

When you're scared, your ears make extra earwax.

Hair grows faster in warmer weather.

Blondes have more hair than people with other hair colors.

WOW!

EVERY DAY YOU LOSE ABOUT 75 STRANDS OF HAIR.

SWEAT, GAS, MUCUS, AND MORE

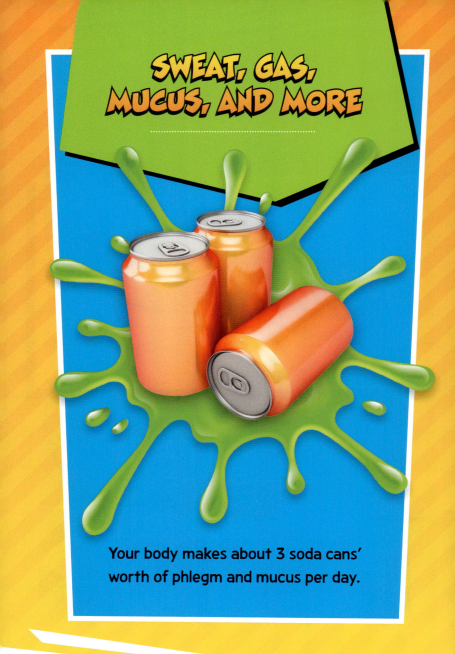

Your body makes about 3 soda cans' worth of phlegm and mucus per day.

You swallow about 1 quart (0.9 L) of snot per day.

Boogers are a sign that your nose is working the way it should.

The bladder is made out of stretchy muscle.

When your bladder is full, it is the size of a grapefruit.

You will poop about 7 tons
(6.4 metric tons) in your lifetime.

A healthy poop should
look like a sausage.

Poop is usually solid and brown, but it is mostly water.

The faster you eat, the more gas you will have.

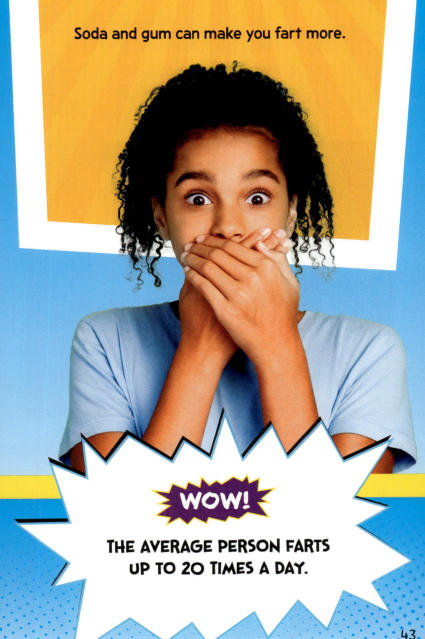

Your stomach is full of acid. It's what breaks down your food.

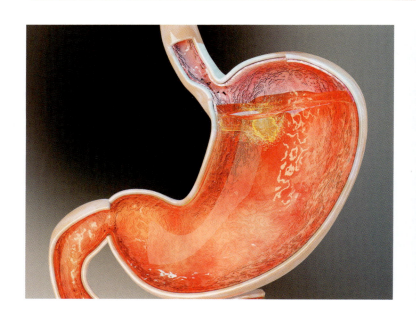

The acid in your stomach is so strong, it can dissolve metal.

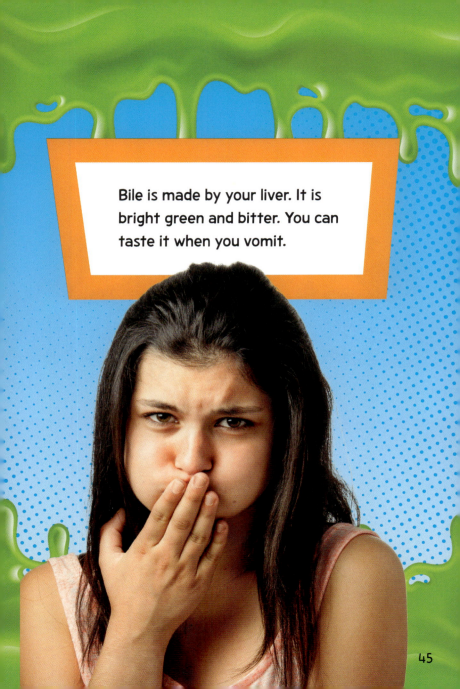

Bile is made by your liver. It is bright green and bitter. You can taste it when you vomit.

The body has 200 types of cells, including those found in blood, skin, and muscles.

50-100 trillion: the number of cells in an adult's body.

You have about 25 trillion red blood cells.

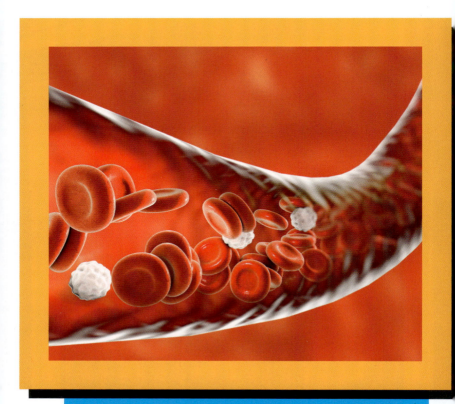

Your body contains about 60,000 miles (96,561 km) of blood vessels!

One drop of blood has about 5 million red blood cells in it.

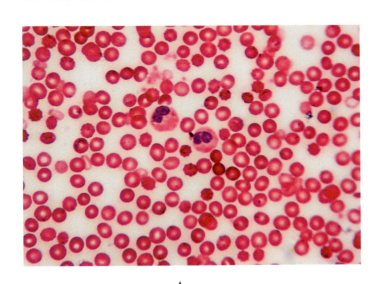

IF A CELL IS DAMAGED OR HAS AN INFECTION, IT SELF-DESTRUCTS.

STRETCH, STAND, MOVE

You are tallest in the morning, because gravity pulls downward on your body throughout the day.

Humans and giraffes have the same number of vertebrae in the neck—seven.

You are born with 33 vertebrae but lose some with age.

You have 206 bones in your body.

The average number of broken bones a person has in a lifetime is two.

A bone can bend, but if bent too much, it will snap.

The femur is the strongest and longest bone in the body. It runs from your hip to your knee.

Your hands and feet have 106 bones.

WOW!

BONES ARE STRONGER THAN CONCRETE.

The hardest working muscle is the heart.

There are 639 muscles in the human body.

The smallest muscles are in your inner ear.

The largest muscle is the gluteus maximus, or your buttocks.

Most of the heat produced in your body comes from muscles contracting.

More than half of the world's population has one foot that is bigger than the other.

There are 500,000 sweat glands in your feet.

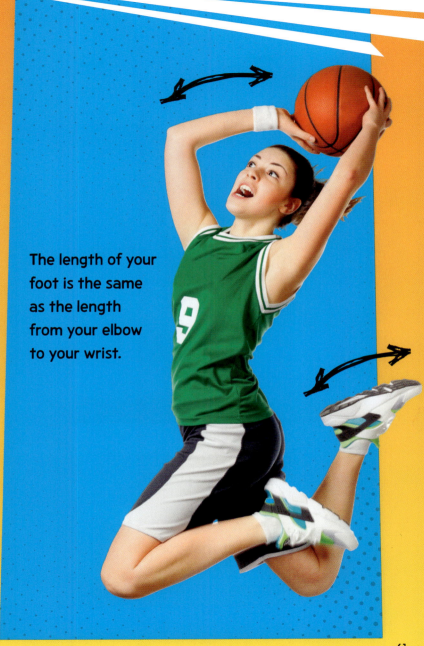

The length of your foot is the same as the length from your elbow to your wrist.

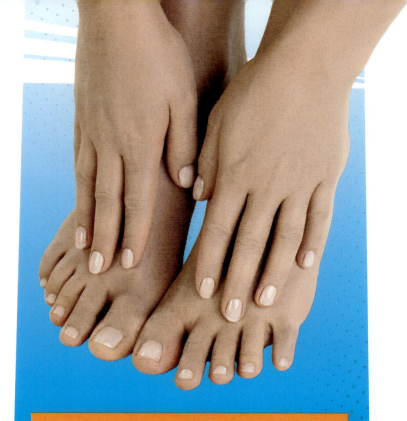

If you lose a finger, a toe can be sewn on to replace it.

Fingernails grow about 3 to 4 times faster than toenails.

If you lose a toenail, it may take one year for it to grow back.

Your thumb is the same size as the length of your nose.

BOOKS IN THIS SERIES